Workplace English

Construction Sites   Hospitals   Doctor's Offices   Grocery Stores

Restaurants   Manufacturing Companies   Office Buildings   Hotels

Ronna Timp

Le: 'loway Lyn .

ISBN 0-9743660-1-3

Printed in the United States of America

First Printing: March 2004

        ͻ6 05 04   6 5 4 3 2 1

        ͻr to order additional books or CDs, visit *www.workplaceesl.com*
        ͻ-3520.

Table of Contents

How do I . . .

Dear Teacher:

In *Workplace English,* employees from construction companies, doctor's offices, grocery stores, hospitals, hotels, restaurants, large or small office buildings, and manufacturing companies will learn to communicate with customers, co-workers and supervisors through authentic workplace conversations. Vocabulary and situations are presented in an easy to follow layout with visual symbols that even the first time language learner can follow. Workplace English focuses on language that is used on a daily basis in workplaces around the world such as:

- Greeting customers
- Giving directions
- Communicating about health
- Reporting accidents and emergencies

A step-by-step teacher's guide presents lesson plans and supplemental activities to help anyone teaching these employees to facilitate a dynamic, engaging and stimulating Workplace ESL class.

Each unit is correlated to CASAS/SCANS competencies. These can be found in the Teacher's Guide.

A CD is available for listening and speaking practice.

For additional information, updates or for questions, visit our website: *www.WorkplaceESL.com* or call (702) 873-3520.

Thank you for trusting us with your learners,

Ronna Timpa
Leslie Holloway
Lyn Pizor

COMMUNICATION GOALS:	Meeting and greeting other people formally and informally
	Spelling your name
	Asking for clarification

 Talking

1. What do you see?
2. What are they saying?

Listening and Speaking

1. Listen
2. Listen and repeat
3. Practice with a partner

José starts a new job today.

José: Hi, my name is **José**. Today is my first day.
Pete: Welcome José. I'm **Pete**. It's nice to meet you.
José: It's nice to meet you, too.

Supervisor: Hello, I'm **Fred**, your supervisor.
José: Hello. It's nice to meet you.
Fred: It's nice to meet you too.
Where are you from?
José: I'm from **Cuba**.
Fred: Your English is good.
José: Thank you. I practice everyday.
Fred: That's great! Well, I'll see you later. It was nice meeting you.
José: You, too. Goodbye.

The next day.

José: Good morning **Pete**. How are you?
Pete: Fine, thanks. How are you?
José: **Great!**

 ## Practice 1

With a partner, practice the conversations using YOUR information.

Matching

Draw a line between the words and the pictures.

Good evening

Fine, thank you.

Good morning

Good bye

I'm from

I'm from Chicago.

Where are you from?

It's nice to meet you.

It's nice to meet you, too.

How are you?

The Alphabet

1. Listen and repeat
2. Practice writing the letters

A a _____

B b _____

C c _____

D d _____

E e _____

F f _____

G g _____

H h _____

I i _____

J j _____

K k _____

L l _____

M m _____

N n _____

O o _____

P p _____

Q q _____

R r _____

S s _____

T t _____

U u _____

V v _____

W w _____

X x _____

Y y _____

Z z _____

A E I O U

Reading

Read the following:

Michael: Good morning, my name is Michael Stockbauer. Today is my first day.

Manager: Can you please spell your last name?

Michael: Sure. It's S-t-o-c-k-b-a-u-e-r.

Manager: Can you please repeat that?

Michael: It's S-t-o-c-k-b-a-u-e-r.

Manager: Can you spell your first name?

Michael: Yes, M-i-c-h-a-e-l.

Manager: Thanks. It's nice to meet you.

Michael: It's nice to meet you, too.

Circle the answer:

1. His first name is Michael.	TRUE	FALSE
2. His last name is Smith.	TRUE	FALSE
3. It is morning.	TRUE	FALSE
4. It is evening.	TRUE	FALSE

Listening

 Circle the appropriate response to the statement or question.

1. A. My name is Ana.

    B. It's nice to meet you.

    C. Fine, thank you.

2. A. Good morning, Sir.

    B. See you tomorrow.

    C. Good evening.

3. A. John

    B. Pete

    C. Ameca

4. A. It's nice to meet you.

    B. See you later.

    C. Good night.

5. A. Stockbauer

    B. Sokoloff

    C. Smith

6. A. María

    B. Mario

    C. Marta

Writing

Write the answers to the following questions:

1. What is your first name?

   _____

2. What is your last name?

   _____

 # Homework

Find three people at your children's school, at the grocery store, or in your neighborhood and practice the following:

1. Hello, my name is _____.

   It's nice to meet you.

2. What is your name?

3. How do you spell it?

4. How are you?

Pronunciation

 Contractions are shortened forms of two words. Listen and repeat.

It is = it's   It's nice to meet you.   It's S-M-I-T-H.

I am = I'm   I'm fine.   I'm OK

 Vocabulary

<u>Verbs</u>	<u>Nouns</u>
to arrive	day
to be	employee
I am	English
He is	evening
She is	manager
You are	morning
We are	name
They are	partner
to get	people
to greet	supervisor
to meet	
to practice	
to repeat	
to see	
to spell	

Fun Activity

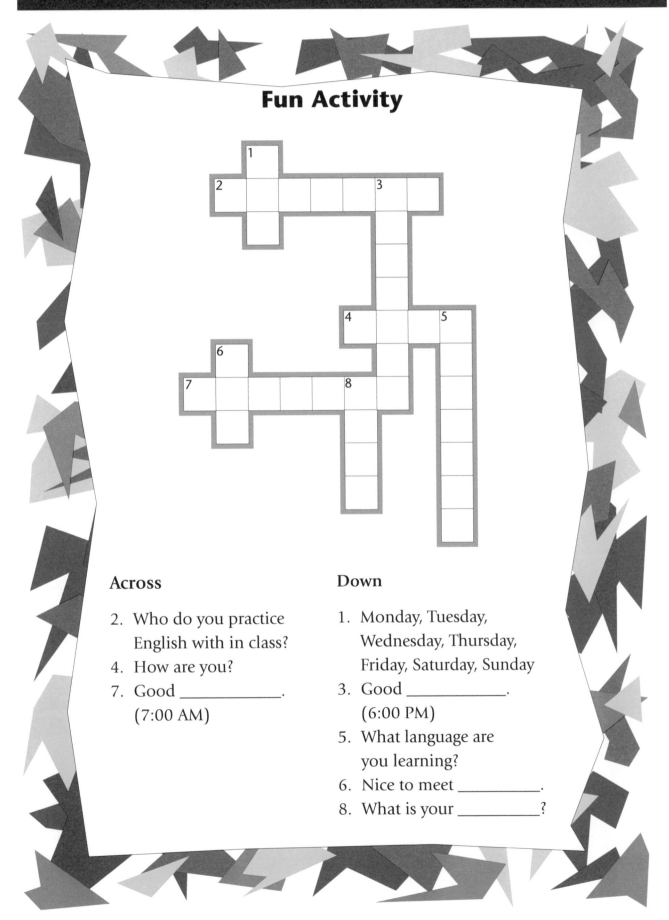

Across

2. Who do you practice English with in class?
4. How are you?
7. Good _____. (7:00 AM)

Down

1. Monday, Tuesday, Wednesday, Thursday, Friday, Saturday, Sunday
3. Good _____. (6:00 PM)
5. What language are you learning?
6. Nice to meet _____.
8. What is your _____?

COMMUNICATION GOALS: Giving personal information

Correctly pronouncing numbers

 Talking

1. What do you see?
2. Where is he?
3. What is he saying?

Listen and Repeat

 The Numbers

0	Zero
1	One
2	Two
3	Three
4	Four
5	Five
6	Six
7	Seven
8	Eight
9	Nine
10	Ten
11	Eleven
12	Twelve
13	Thirteen
14	Fourteen
15	Fifteen
16	Sixteen
17	Seventeen
18	Eighteen
19	Nineteen
20	Twenty
30	Thirty
40	Forty
50	Fifty
60	Sixty
70	Seventy
80	Eighty
90	Ninety
100	One Hundred

Listening and Speaking

 1. **Listen**
2. **Listen and Repeat**
3. **Practice with a partner**

Sarah:	Hello, my name is Sarah Allen.
Receptionist:	Good morning, Miss Allen. Do you have an appointment?
Sarah:	Yes, at 10:00.
Receptionist:	Ok. Could you spell your first name, please?
Patient:	Yes, it's S-A-R-A-H.
Receptionist:	And your last name?
Patient:	Sure. It's A-L-L-E-N
Receptionist:	And your date of birth?
Patient:	4/9/59
Receptionist:	Thank you. Please fill out this form.

Name		
Last	**First**	**Middle**
Allen	Sarah	A.

Address				
Number	**Street**	**City**	**State**	**Zip code**
516	Gibson St.	Las Vegas	NV	89015

Phone	**Birth date**	**Age**
702-324-8854	10/02/78	25

Social Security Number
123-45-6789

Matching

Draw a line between the words and the pictures.

First name	123-45-6789
Birthdate	89128
Address	CA
City	(702) 325-8854
Zipcode	Las Vegas
Social Security Number	4/9/02
State	Sarah
Phone number	*Sarah Allen*
Signature	2227 Schiller Street

Practice 1

In pairs, role play. One person is the patient and the other is the receptionist. Use your personal information:

1. How do you spell your first name?
2. What's your date of birth?
3. What's your telephone number?
4. What's your address?
5. What's your zipcode?
6. What's your last name? Can you spell that?

Reading

Read the following:

Sarah Allen does not feel well. She has an appointment with the doctor at 10:00 AM. The receptionist needs information from Sarah for their medical records.

Answer the following questions:

1. Sarah doesn't feel well.   TRUE   FALSE
2. Sarah is the patient's last name.   TRUE   FALSE
3. Sarah's appointment is at 10:00.   TRUE   FALSE
4. The receptionist needs information from Sarah. TRUE   FALSE

Listening Activity

 Circle the appropriate response to the statement or question that you hear:

1. A. Yes, it is my first day.
   B. It's 456-6776
   C. Yes, at 2:00.

2. A. It's 5/3/76
   B. It's 474-58-5522
   C. It's (702) 888-6633

3. A. Yes, it's G R E E N E.
   B. Yes, it's G R E Y.
   C. Yes, it's G R A N T.

4. A. It's 810-2161
   B. Nevada
   C. Sarah

5. A. 320-52-1020
   B. 7/16/62
   C. (310) 555-1313

6. A. S-A-R-A-H
   B. 307 Rawhide Street
   C. U.S.A

 Writing

Fill out this form with YOUR information. Practice saying this information after you write it.

Name		
Last	**First**	**Middle**

Address				
Number	**Street**	**City**	**State**	**Zip code**

Phone	Birth date	Age

Social Security Number

Homework

Practice saying your son's, daughter's, husband's, wife's or friend's personal information with good pronunciation. Include his or her first and last name, his or her address, and phone number with area code. Then practice spelling the same names. Practice spelling the name of your street.

  ## Pronunciation

 1. Listen and repeat
2. Listen again. Circle the number you hear.

1. 13 30
2. 14 40
3. 15 50
4. 16 60

5. 17 70
6. 18 80
7. 19 90

Vocabulary

Verbs

to give
to spell
to fill out
to need
to pronounce

Nouns

address
appointment
city
date of birth
doctor
female
first name
form

male
medical records
patient
receptionist
signature
social security number
state
telephone number

Fun Activity

Across

1. 6
4. 4
5. 2
7. 19
11. 13
12. 60
13. 18
15. 30
16. 9
18. 8
19. 14
21. 16
22. 12
23. 7
24. 10

Down

1. 17
2. 50
3. 5
4. 40
6. 20
8. 80
9. 11
10. 15
14. 90
17. 3
20. 1
21. 70

COMMUNICATION GOALS: Telling time

Communicating daily work schedules

 Talking

1. What do you see?
2. What are they doing?
3. Where are they?

Listening and Speaking

1. Listen
2. Listen and repeat
3. Practice with a partner

A patient is talking with a nurse in a hospital.

Patient: What time is lunch?
Nurse: In an hour. At 12:30.
Patient: I'm hungry NOW!
Nurse: OK. I can get you some crackers in five minutes.
Patient: Thank you.
Nurse: You're welcome.

A man wants his office cleaned.

Man: Hello, can you please clean my office now?
Janitor: I can clean it in a half hour. I have to finish the restroom first.
Man: OK. Can you have it finished by a quarter after 2?
Janitor: Yes, it will be finished by 2:15.
Man: Thank you. I have a meeting at 2:30.
Janitor: No problem!

Matching

Match the clock to the correct time:

1.    It's 1:00 AM.

2.    It's 11:20 PM.

3.    It's 8:45 AM.

4.    It's 2:15 AM.

5.    It's 1:50 PM.

6.    It's 9:30 AM.

Practice 1

Make a conversation with another person. Use these clock times.

A: What time do you start work?

B: I clock in at _____.

1.    4.

2.    5.

3.    6.

Reading

Read the following:

Matt and Adam work for Watson Construction Company. They start work at 8:00 AM. They clock in at 7:55 AM. They clock out for their lunch break at noon and clock in at 1:00 PM. They finish work at 5:00 PM and clock out.

Answer the following questions:

1. Matt and Adam work in a restaurant.   TRUE   FALSE

2. Matt needs to clock in at 8:00 AM.   TRUE   FALSE

3. Adam has a lunch break from 12:00 – 1:00 PM.   TRUE   FALSE

4. They finish work at 4:00 PM.   TRUE   FALSE

Practice 2

In pairs, ask your partner about his or her work schedule.

What time do you clock in and clock out?

What time do you eat lunch?

What time do you go home?

  Listening

Circle the appropriate response to the statement or question that you hear:

1. A. at 8:15

    B. fifteen minute breaks

    C. 7:00 – 3:00

2. A. 8:00 – 4:00

    B. 10 minutes

    C. at 12:30

3. A. 2:30

    B. 3:30

    C. 3:13

4. A. 4:00 PM

    B. 8:00 PM

    C. 4:08 AM

Writing

Write the answers to the following questions:

1. What time do you start work?

    _____

2. How long is your lunch break?

    _____

3. What time is lunch?

    _____

4. What time do you clock out?

    _____

 ## Homework

Ask 3 people the questions listed below. Write down their answers.

	Person 1	Person 2	Person 3
What time do you start work?			
What time is your lunch break?			
What time do you finish work?			

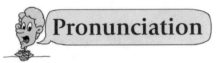

Pronunciation

1. Listen and repeat
2. Listen and circle the time you hear

Times:	1. 12:50 12:15	3. 2:30 2:13	5. 5:40 5:14
	2. 3:13 3:30	4. 6:55 6:05	6. 8:15 8:45

1. Listen and repeat
2. Listen and circle the date you hear

Dates:	7. 1960 1916	9. 1970 1917	11. 1990 1919
	8. 2004 2040	10. 2015 2050	12. 2018 2008

Vocabulary

Verbs	Nouns
to clock in	break
to eat	breakfast
to finish	crackers
to get up	dinner
to go	home
to help	hospital
to start	lunch
to take	minute
to watch	nurse
to work	patient
	restaurant
	time
	work

Fun Activity

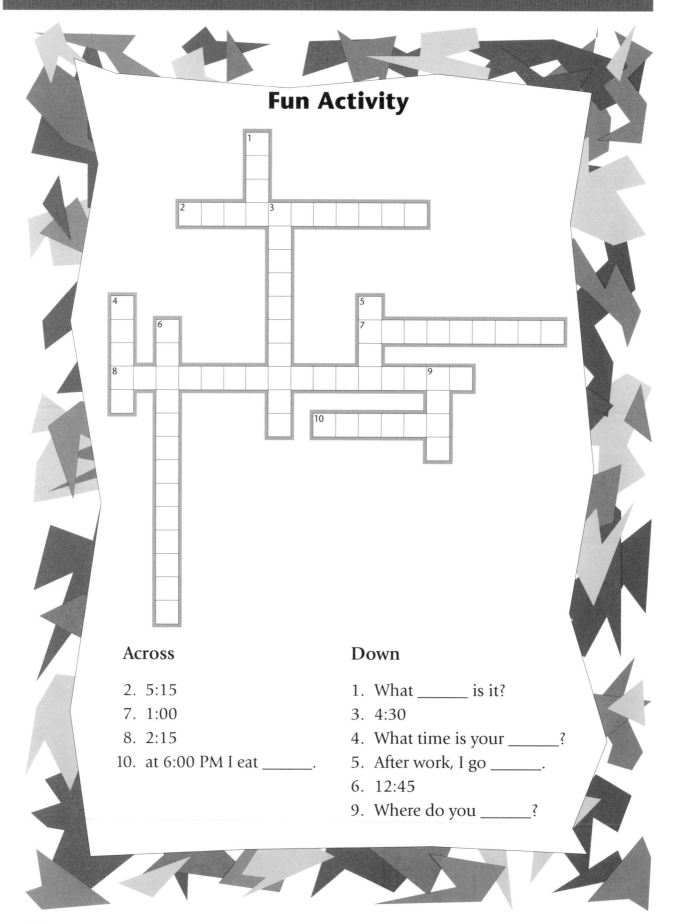

Across

2. 5:15
7. 1:00
8. 2:15
10. at 6:00 PM I eat _____.

Down

1. What _____ is it?
3. 4:30
4. What time is your _____?
5. After work, I go _____.
6. 12:45
9. Where do you _____?

COMMUNICATION GOALS:	Communicating information about a work schedule
	Recognizing commonly paid holidays

December

Sunday	Monday	Tuesday	Wednesday	Thursday	Friday	Saturday
	1 OFF	2	3	4	5	6
7 OFF	8 OFF	9	10	11	12	13
14 OFF	15 OFF	16	17	18	19	20
21 OFF	22 OFF	23	24	25	26	27
28 OFF	29 OFF	30	31			

 Talking

1. What do you see?
2. What are the days of the week?
3. What day is Christmas?
4. How many weeks are there in December?

Listening and Speaking

 1. Listen
2. Listen and repeat
3. Practice with a partner

Stuart: When do you start your new job, Margi?

Margi: On April 15th.

Stuart: What day of the week is that?

Margi: That's a Monday. What days do you work?

Stuart: I work Wednesday to Sunday. My days off are Monday and Tuesday.

Margi: Where do you work?

Stuart: I work at Jason's Supermarket. Where will you be working?

Margi: My new job is at Rush Hospital.

April						
Sunday	Monday	Tuesday	Wednesday	Thursday	Friday	Saturday
				1	2	3
4	5	6	7	8	9	10
11	12	13	14	15	16	17
18	19	20	21	22	23	24
25	26	27	28	29	30	

Practice 1

Practice asking and answering these questions with a partner.

1. What day of the week is April 2?
2. What is the date on the first Sunday of the month?
3. What day of the week is April 11th?
4. What days of the week does Stuart work?
5. What are Stuart's days off?
6. Where does Stuart work?
7. Where is Margi's new job?

Reading

Read the following:

Today is March 28. Tomorrow is my birthday. I will be 35 years old. My family is having a big birthday party for me. We will eat chicken and have birthday cake. I have to work today, but I have tomorrow off.

Answer the following questions:

1.	Today is my birthday.	TRUE	FALSE
2.	I have to work tomorrow.	TRUE	FALSE
3.	We will eat pizza tomorrow.	TRUE	FALSE
4.	I am 35 years old today.	TRUE	FALSE
5.	I have tomorrow off.	TRUE	FALSE

Matching

In January and February it is cold.

In March it's windy.

In April it rains a lot.

In May there are flowers.

In June, many people get married.

In July, we take vacations.

In August it's hot.

In September and October it's cloudy.

In November there is a lot of fog.

In December it snows.

Listening

 Circle the appropriate response to the statement or question that you hear:

1. A. April 13th
   B. 8:00 pm
   C. April 30th

2. A. January
   B. February
   C. March

3. A. I don't work on Monday.
   B. I don't work on Wednesday.
   C. I don't work on Saturday.

4. A. September
   B. Wednesday
   C. 3:00 PM

5. A. April 1, 2002
   B. April 5, 2004
   C. April 15, 1998

6. A. On Tuesday
   B. At the hospital
   C. On September 13th

Writing

Write the answers to the following questions with your information:

1. Where do you work?

   _____

2. What day is it today?

   _____

3. What is today's date?

   _____

4. When is your birthday?

   _____

Homework

Ask three people these questions.

	NAME	ANSWER
When is your birthday?		
Where do you work?		
What are your days off?		

 Pronunciation

To pronounce the "th", place your tongue between your teeth.

Practice saying the following words. Listen and repeat:

think	thumb	Thursday	thank you	bathtub	
Fourth	fifth	sixth	seventh	eighth	ninth
Tenth	eleventh	twelfth	birthday	month	

Now try these sentences. Listen and repeat:

Thank you for being so thoughtful.

I think so.

Today is the third Thursday of the month.

That's right!

It's Thursday, not Tuesday.

Vocabulary

Verbs

to have

Months

January
February
March
April
May
June
July
August
September
October
November
December

Days of the week

Sunday
Monday
Tuesday
Wednesday
Thursday
Friday
Saturday

Ordinal numbers

first
second
third
fourth
fifth
sixth
seventh
eighth
ninth
tenth
eleventh
twelfth

Other Nouns

birthday
date
day
days off
month
party
today
tomorrow
week
year

Fun Activity

Word Search

January	February	March	April	May
June	July	August	September	October
November	December	Sunday	Monday	Tuesday
Wednesday	Thursday	Friday	Saturday	

```
r  u  n  o  v  e  m  b  e  r  z  v  k  z  v
u  e  w  h  g  c  f  t  h  u  r  s  d  a  y
d  e  c  e  m  b  e  r  a  g  a  j  u  l  y
e  s  o  c  t  o  b  e  r  t  a  r  s  e  x
l  a  z  m  a  y  f  r  i  d  a  y  a  t  n
j  z  t  u  e  s  d  a  y  m  g  v  p  i  k
p  p  m  a  r  c  h  q  b  b  p  l  r  i  r
d  z  u  e  s  u  n  d  a  y  l  d  i  r  s
d  r  d  y  p  j  a  n  u  a  r  y  l  f  b
o  p  e  s  e  p  t  e  m  b  e  r  c  w  t
d  l  p  p  f  e  b  r  u  a  r  y  p  u  e
c  k  a  w  e  d  n  e  s  d  a  y  w  q  e
g  a  u  g  u  s  t  c  h  m  o  n  d  a  y
x  q  a  j  u  n  e  s  a  t  u  r  d  a  y
v  n  r  i  q  l  h  c  d  l  n  e  m  d  c
```

COMMUNICATION GOALS:

Making an appointment

Describing symptoms

Making suggestions

Calling in sick

Filling out a patient information form

 # Talking

1. What do you see?
2. Where are they?
3. What are they saying?
4. What are they doing?

Listening and Speaking

 1. **Listen**
2. **Listen and repeat**
3. **Practice with a partner**

Doctor's Office:	Hello, Dr. Kent's Office.
Patient:	Hi. This is Niah Riggs.
	I'd like to make an appointment.
Doctor's Office:	Have you been here before?
Niah:	Yes.
Doctor's Office:	What is your date of birth?
Niah:	It's 10/3/62
Doctor's Office:	Ok. Why do you need to see Dr. Kent?
Niah:	I have diarrhea, a sore throat and a fever of 104.
Doctor's Office:	Can you come in at 1:30 today?
Niah:	Yes.
Doctor's Office:	Please bring your insurance card and a picture ID.
Niah:	I will.

Supervisor's Office:	Hello?
Niah :	Hello. May I speak to Paul?
Supervisor's Office:	Yes, one moment please.
Paul:	Hello, this is Paul.
Niah :	Hello Paul, this is Niah. I can't come to work today because I'm sick.
Paul:	What is wrong?
Niah :	I have diarrhea, a sore throat and a fever.
Paul:	OK. Will you be back tomorrow?
Niah :	I'll call you tomorrow morning and let you know. I'm going to the doctor today at 1:30.
Paul:	Feel better.

Matching

Match the illnesses to the pictures:

I have a stomachache.

I have a fever.

I have a sore throat.

I have an earache.

I have the flu.

I hurt my back.

I hurt my leg.

Listen and Repeat

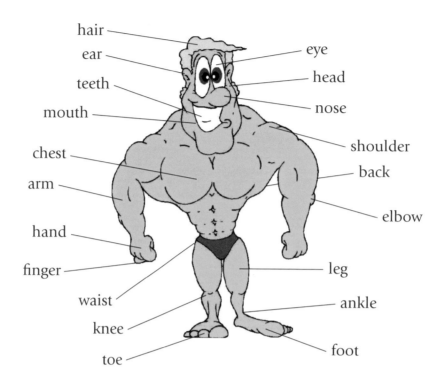

hair — eye

ear — head

teeth — nose

mouth

chest — shoulder

arm — back

hand — elbow

finger

waist — leg

knee — ankle

toe — foot

Practice with a partner. Tell what hurts.

I hurt my _____.

or

My _____ hurt(s).

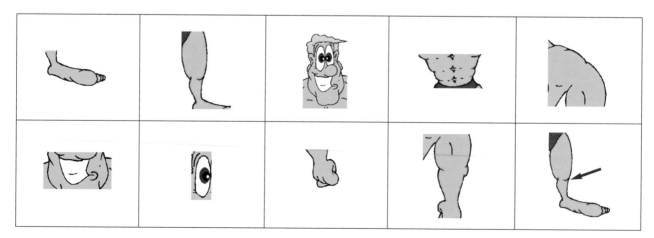

Practice 1

In pairs, make a conversation describing an illness to a friend. Fill in the blanks with vocabulary from the words below.

A. Hi, (name). How are you today?

B. I feel (A).

A. What's wrong?

B. My (any body part) hurts and I have a (B).

A. I'm sorry to hear that.

B. I've been sick for (any number) days.

A. You should (C) and (C).

Vocabulary Bank:

A: terrible	B: stomachache	C: call the doctor
sick	headache	take aspirin
better	sore throat	rest
	earache	drink a lot of liquids
	backache	stay in bed
		rest

 # Practice 2

In pairs, role play. One of you is the supervisor and the other is the employee.

1. Call in sick. Tell what is wrong.

2. Call to say that your child is sick and you cannot come to work.

3. Tell your supervisor that you are sick and need to leave work early.

Reading

Read the following:

Brian feels terrible today. He can't go to work. Brian has a headache, stomachache and a sore throat. He has been sick for 3 days. Brian needs to take medicine and drink a lot of water. He should stay in bed.

Answer the following: Circle True or False

1. Brian has been sick for a day.   TRUE   FALSE

2. He has a headache and sore throat.   TRUE   FALSE

3. Brian has a job.   TRUE   FALSE

4. Brian has a broken arm.   TRUE   FALSE

5. He needs to rest and drink a lot of coffee. TRUE   FALSE

Listening

 Circle the appropriate response to the statement or question that you hear:

1. A. My head hurts.

   B. My stomach hurts.

   C. My leg hurts.

5. A.

   B.

2. A. It's Monday.

   B. My baby is sick.

   C. Today at 4:00.

6. A.

   B.

3. A. I will be late.

   B. I hurt my arm.

   C. Thank you.

7. A.

   B.

4. A. I'm sorry to hear that.

   B. Goodbye.

   C. Thank you.

8. A.

   B.

41

Writing

Fill out the New Patient Form with YOUR information.

New Patient Form

Name _____

Address _____

Telephone (H) _____ (W) _____

Date of Birth _____   Male / Female   Insurance   YES   NO

Name of Insurance Company _____

Medical Problem _____

Homework

Make a list of important phone numbers for you and your family. Practice calling in sick for your family members.

Emergency Numbers

Supervisor: _____

Family Doctor: _____

Neighbor: _____

Family Friend or Relative: _____

Pronunciation

The silent "e" at the end of a word makes the first vowel "long." The "e" is not pronounced and a consonant is actually the last sound.

Listen and Repeat:

pet / Pete	tub / tube	pin / pine
kit / kite	cap / cape	slid / slide
Sam / same	Tim / time	cod / code

Vocabulary

<u>Verbs</u>	<u>Body parts</u>	<u>Other Nouns</u>
to drink	ankle	ambulance
to rest	arm	cold
to stay	back	diarrhea
to take	chest	doctor
	ear	earache
	elbow	fever
	eye	fire
	finger	flu
	foot	friend
	hair	headache
	hand	medicine
	head	neighbor
	heart	police
	hip	sore throat
	knee	stomachache
	leg	
	lips	
	mouth	
	neck	
	nose	
	shoulder	
	stomach	
	throat	
	toe	
	wrist	

Fun Activities

1. Write a description of an outer space creature. Use your imagination! (Ask your teacher for help.) Read it to another person and ask that person to draw the creature that you have described.

   _____

   _____

   _____

   _____

2. Fill in the blanks with the correct vocabulary word from the list:

   Vocabulary List

Head	Legs	Arms	Fingers	Hand
Nose	Stomach	Ears	Neck	Mouth

   A hat is for your _____.

   We use our _____ to speak.

   We hold a pen in our _____ to write.

   I wear a scarf around my _____.

   We hear with our _____.

   When we sleep, we close our _____.

   In order to swim, we move our _____ and

   _____.

   We smell beautiful flowers with our _____.

   We have 5 _____ on each hand.

   We put food in our mouths and it goes to our _____.

COMMUNICATION GOALS:	Taking food orders
	Using polite language with customers
	Giving good customer service

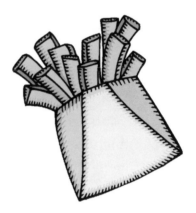

 Talking

1. What do you see?
2. Where is she?
3. What are they saying?

Listening and Speaking

 1. Listen
   2. Listen and repeat
   3. Practice with a partner

Cashier: Good afternoon. Welcome to ABC Burger. What can I get for you today?

Customer: Combo #3 with a diet cola.

Cashier: Would you like anything else?

Customer: Yes, I would also like an order of french fries.

Cashier: OK, that's one #3 with an order of french fries and a diet cola. Would you like to add a salad or ice cream for 99 cents?

Customer: No, thank you.

Cashier: OK. That's $5.70. Out of $10? Your change is $4.30. Your order number is 87.

Customer: Thank you. Can I have extra napkins and some ketchup please?

Cashier: Sure. Here's your order. Come again!

◆ HAMBURGER   ◆ FRENCH FRIES
◆ DBLE HAMBURGER   ◆ ONION RINGS
◆ CHEESEBURGER   ◆ SUNDAES
◆ DBLE CHEESEBURGER   ◆ FLOATS
◆ HOT DOG   ◆ MILKSHAKES
◆ DBLE HOT DOG   ◆ ICE CREAM

Customer: Excuse me, you are out of forks and knives.

Cashier: OK. I'll refill all the silverware, including the spoons.

Customer: Great. Thank you.

Matching

Draw a line from the word to the correct picture:

Cash register

Menu

French fries

Hamburger

Salad

Diet Cola

Ice Cream

Ketchup

Silverware

Napkin

Practice 1

Role play

Practice with a partner. Imagine you are at a fast food restaurant. One of you will be the customer and the other the cashier. Use the dialog on page 46. Make a conversation with your partner. See the pictures below to decide what you will order.

Reading

Yesterday, John went to ABC Burger. He ordered a coffee at the drive thru window. After he left, he tried the coffee and it was cold. John went back to ABC Burger and told the cashier his coffee was cold. He asked for his money back because he was angry. ABC Burger gave him a refund and said SORRY!!

Circle True or False below.

1. John purchased a diet cola.	TRUE	FALSE
2. The coffee was hot.	TRUE	FALSE
3. John went back to ABC Burger.	TRUE	FALSE
4. John will not get a refund.	TRUE	FALSE
5. John bought another cup of coffee.	TRUE	FALSE

Listening

 Circle the correct answer based on what you hear on the CD.

1. A.

   B.

   C.

4. A.

   B.

   C.

2. A. $8.75

   B. $6.25

   C. $5.50

5. A.

   B.

   C.

3. A. Yes, please.

   B. No, thank you.

   C. O.K.

 Writing

You are the owner of _____'s (insert your name) Burgers. Write the menu. Write all the food items and prices of everything you will sell. Ask a friend or one of your children for ideas for your restaurant.

Menu

_____'s Burgers

Item	Price
_____	_____
_____	_____
_____	_____
_____	_____
_____	_____

 Homework

Go to a fast food restaurant and order french fries and a drink in English. OR practice ordering food with a family member or friend. Where did you go? What did you order? Who did you practice with?

Where   _____

What   _____

Who   _____

Pronunciation

Verbs with **–ed** endings may be pronounced three different ways. /**d**/, /**t**/, /**id**/.

/d/

The supervisor stay**ed** at work all night.

The kitchen worker clean**ed** the walls and stove.

He fill**ed** out the form for the doctor.

Mary spell**ed** her last name.

/t/

Silvia laugh**ed** at the joke.

The cook look**ed** for a clean pot.

The customer purchas**ed** a hamburger.

John finish**ed** work at 5:00.

/id/

José wait**ed** for his paycheck.

He need**ed** ID to cash his check.

The restaurant refund**ed** his money.

She repeat**ed** the question.

Vocabulary

Verbs
to buy
to purchase
to refund

Nouns
bacon
cash register
cola
combo

customer
diet cola
eggs
fork
french fries
hamburger
hot dog
ice cream
ketchup
knife

menu
milk
napkin
pizza
refund
salad
sandwich
spoon
taco

Fun Activity

Word Search

bacon   napkin   sandwich   milk   hot dog
cash register   pizza   spoon   menu   ice cream
customer   refund   fork   knife   hamburger
cola   salad   taco   ketchup   eggs

```
y q p c o l a y a x k n i f e
c a s h r e g i s t e r g d q
g w u k t a c o q m i l k p g
f x j t f s p o o n p e n u m
n h a m b u r g e r n g s f f
z i c e c r e a m e a g b o c
k b y n v l m e n u p s u r o
s a n d w i c h m q k c l k n
l i f b a c o n x l i u s g d
l k g a o p i z z a n s w i b
t x s s h o t d o g n t s e f
c c i d x s a l a d b o w o s
k e t c h u p q z u e m x g p
z j u v y r e f u n d e m u l
l a g j u e s w b l y r u x l
```

COMMUNICATION GOALS:	Talking about cleaning responsibilities
	Reporting problems
	Following instructions

 ## Talking

What do you see?
What are they doing?
Where are they?

Listening and Speaking

 1. **Listen**
2. **Listen and repeat**
3. **Practice with a partner**

Supervisor: Jay, please take the mop and
bucket to the restroom and mop
up the wet floor. The toilet overflowed.

Employee: OK, I'll go right now.

Supervisor: When you finish, please replace the
paper towels, soap and toilet paper.
Then, empty the trashcans. Next, clean
the toilets and wipe the sinks. Finally,
please clean the mirrors.

Employee: No problem.

Matching

Draw a line from the word to the correct picture.

mop

bucket

toilet

paper towels

soap

toilet paper

sink

broom

vacuum

trashcan

Practice 1

Your supervisor asks you to clean an office. Make a conversation asking what you should do.

Supervisor: (Name), you need to clean the office on the 2nd floor.

Employee: What should I do?

Supervisor: First, _____.

Then, _____.

Finally, _____.

Employee: OK, I understand. First, I _____.

Then, I _____ and finally,

I _____.

Supervisor: That's correct. Thank you.

Employee: No problem.

Reading

Read and answer the questions.

I need to clean the office. First, I will empty the trashcan. Then, I will dust and vacuum. Last, I will wipe the mirrors and computers.

1. What will I do first?
    A. dust
    B. wipe mirrors
    C. empty the trashcan

2. When will I dust?
    A. first
    B. second
    C. third

3. What will I wipe?
    A. the mirrors and computers
    B. the trashcan
    C. the floor

4. Where will I put the trash?
    A. in the vacuum
    B. on the floor
    C. in the trashcan

Listening

 Listen to the CD and pick the correct picture.

1. A.

   B.

   C.

3. A.

   B.

   C.

2. A.

   B.

   C.

4. A.

   B.

   C.

Practice 2

Look at each picture and make a conversation with a partner about reporting the problem.

Example: Employee: Maintenance, there is a stopped up toilet in room 324.

Maintenance: Thank you. I'll send someone to fix it right away.

1.

2.

3.

4.

Writing

What are they doing? Write a sentence describing their actions.

Example:  <u>He is mopping the floor.</u>

1. _____

2.  _____

3. _____

4.  _____

5.  _____

6.  _____

Homework

Make a list of things that need to be cleaned. What will you use to clean them?

Needs to be cleaned	What do you use to clean it?
_____	_____
_____	_____
_____	_____
_____	_____

 Pronunciation

 "**SH**" is a quiet, steady sound....SHHHHH!

Listen and Repeat:

fini**sh**   **sh**ine   **sh**elf   ru**sh**

tra**sh**   di**sh**   wa**sh**   wa**sh**ing machine

Listen and repeat the following sentences:

What **sh**ould I do first?

When will you fini**sh** that job?

Please **sh**ut the door when you fini**sh** cleaning the room.

Wa**sh** the di**sh**es in the di**sh**wa**sh**er.

Vocabulary

 Verbs

to bring
to change
to clean
to dust
to empty
to finish
to mix
to mop
to put
to replace
to sweep
to vacuum
to wash
to wipe

Nouns

broom
bucket
computer
dishwasher
dust pan
machine
mirror
mop
paper towels
restroom
sink
soap
spill
toilet
toilet paper
vacuum
window cleaner
window

Fun Activity

Unscramble the letters to make a word.

morob
_____

ubkect
_____

rtomceup
_____

ehsardshiw
_____

tdus apn
_____

aneihcm
_____

omp
_____

rmriro
_____

pepra setlow
_____

tooerrsm
_____

insk
_____

paos
_____

lilps
_____

tileto
_____

acuvum
_____

ondwiw
_____

COMMUNICATION GOALS:	Asking for and give directions
	Talking about locations

 # Talking

1. What do you see?
2. Where are they?
3. What are they saying?

Listening and Speaking

1. Listen
2. Listen and repeat
3. Practice with a partner

Man in car:	Excuse me. Where is the closest gas station?
Construction worker:	It's on the corner of First Street and Green Avenue.
Man in car:	How do I get there from here?
Construction worker:	Go straight, past the post office. Turn left at the corner. The gas sation is next to the library.
Man in car:	Turn right at the corner?
Construction worker:	No. Left at the corner.
Man in car:	Thank you very much.
Construction worker:	You're welcome.

Matching

Match the vocabulary to the pictures:

turn left

turn right

go straight

across

next to

on the corner

behind

on

between

Practice 1

In pairs, make a conversation. Use the conversation as your model. The location for each place is shown below:

A. Excuse me. How do I get to _____?

1.

3.

5.

2.

4.

6.

B. Go that way. It's _____.

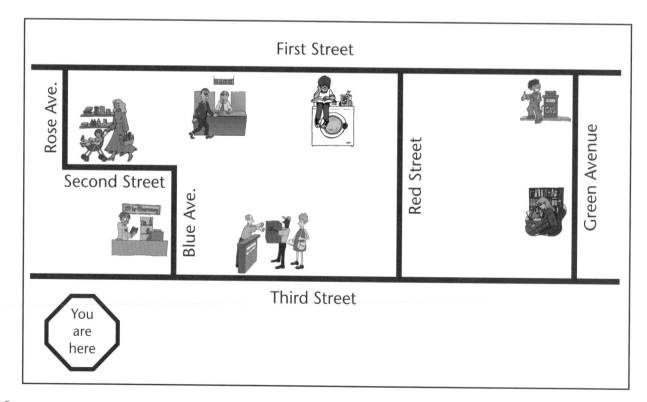

Reading

Read the following:

Mark works at the gas station. Paula is attending an English class at 2:00 PM at the library. She needs directions. Mark tells Paula that the library is downtown on Main Street. It is next to the police station and across from the park.

Answer the following questions:

1.	Mark and Paula are going to the library.	TRUE	FALSE
2.	Paula is studying Chinese.	TRUE	FALSE
3.	The library is next to the park.	TRUE	FALSE
4.	The police station is next to the library.	TRUE	FALSE
5.	English class is at 2:00 PM.	TRUE	FALSE

Practice 2

Role Play. Practice giving directions to a partner.

1. Give directions to Human Resources from your work station.

2. Give directions to a restroom from your work station.

3. Give directions to the cafeteria from your work station.

4. Give directions to your house to a co-worker because you are having a party.

Listening

Listen to the CD. Follow the directions that are given and write the name of the building that you come to after following the directions. Use the map and follow the directions that you hear. Where are you?

1. _____

2. _____

3. _____

4. _____

5. _____

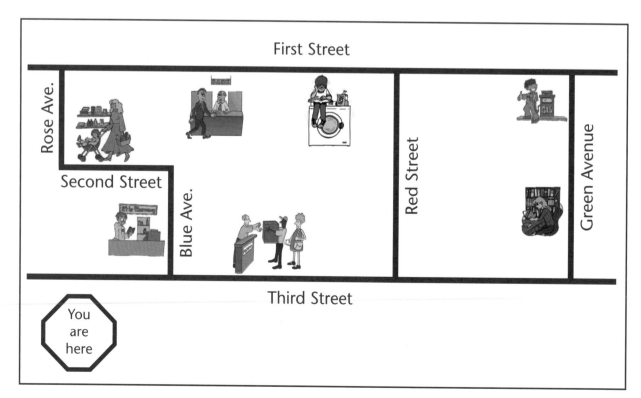

Writing

Write the answers to the following questions:

1. Where is a library? _____

2. What street do you work on? _____

3. Where is Human Resources? _____

4. Where is a bank? _____

 # Homework

Draw a map of your neighborhood. Where is the nearest grocery store? Where is your bank? Where is the park? Be prepared to practice giving directions with a partner when you bring your map to class.

 **Pronunciation**

 The letters "L" and "R"

To pronounce the letter "L", your tongue touches the ridge of your gum. Listen and repeat making sure that you place your tongue against your gum.

late   led   library   elect   label   left

To pronounce the letter "R", never allow your tongue to touch your upper gum ridge. Listen and repeat making sure that the tip of your tongue does NOT touch the roof of your mouth.

drug store   red   row   erect   right   read

Practice these pairs of words. Concentrate on the correct pronunciation of the letters "L" and "R". Listen and repeat:

light/right   collect/correct   lock/rock   play/pray   clash/crash

---

 Vocabulary

 Verbs
to take

Nouns
bank

directions

downtown

drug store

gas station

grocery store

laundromat

library

movie theater

park

police station

post office

school

Fun Activity

Word Search

bank   directions   school   gas station   movie theater
grocery store   park   laundromat   drug store
library   police station   post office   downtown

```
j  z  g  r  o  c  e  r  y  s  t  o  r  e  k
e  d  o  w  n  t  o  w  n  i  t  q  h  e  a
a  p  o  s  t  o  f  f  i  c  e  t  e  z  l
o  l  j  d  i  r  e  c  t  i  o  n  s  h  x
q  p  t  u  c  d  t  j  a  i  x  u  c  a  t
r  d  r  u  g  s  t  o  r  e  h  f  k  q  e
z  p  o  l  i  c  e  s  t  a  t  i  o  n  y
l  i  b  r  a  r  y  r  l  s  c  h  o  o  l
s  f  s  l  a  u  n  d  r  o  m  a  t  e  g
j  m  o  v  i  e  t  h  e  a  t  e  r  o  s
m  q  l  g  k  w  l  b  c  c  d  p  p  j  q
a  u  m  v  q  d  t  g  b  a  n  k  r  s  o
o  p  g  a  s  s  t  a  t  i  o  n  l  r  p
a  d  k  h  i  p  a  r  k  t  b  r  p  f  n
i  t  p  c  q  h  n  f  m  h  z  p  q  d  t
```

COMMUNICATION GOALS:
Describing physical characteristics

Reporting accidents

Describing emergency situations

 Talking

1. What do you see?
2. Where are they?
3. What are they saying?

Listening and Speaking

 1. **Listen**
   2. **Listen and repeat**
   3. **Practice with a partner**

911 Operator: 911 Emergency . . .
        Tim: Hello? There's been a car accident!
              We need an ambulance.
911 Operator: Where are you?
        Tim: At Watson Construction. On the
              corner of Elm Street and Glenn Drive.
911 Operator: The police and ambulance are on their way.
        Tim: Thank you.

Supervisor: Hello?
      John: Help!!! A customer slipped
           on the wet floor.
Supervisor: Is he hurt?
      John: Yes. I think he broke his leg.
Supervisor: OK. I'll call an ambulance.
      John: Thanks.

Security: Hello?
    Jack: Help. There is a big fight in
         front of the men's restroom.
Security: OK. I'll send security right now.
         Thank you.

Matching

Match the words to the pictures:

Police

Fire

Fire Extinguisher

Men's Restroom

Women's Restroom

Car accident

Fight

Robbery

Heart attack

Practice 1

Role Play. One person is a 911 operator or the security department (depending on who you call from work) . The other person is reporting the situation.

Example:

911 Operator or Security:	911 emergency or Security . . .
Employee:	Help. There is a fire in the office.
Security:	Is anybody hurt?
Employee:	No, but hurry.
Security:	OK. I'll call the fire department right now.
Employee:	Thanks.

1.

3.

2.

4.

Reading

Read the following:

Tony works in a grocery store. He is a cashier. There are several people shopping. A man approaches María and takes her purse. The thief runs out of the store. María tells Tony that a man just stole her purse. Tony dials 911. The police are on their way. When the police arrive, María describes the man. He is heavy, he is wearing a pink shirt and a yellow hat, and is wearing sunglasses.

Find the man described in the reading and circle his picture.

Answer the following questions:

1. Tony is a stock boy at the grocery store.	TRUE	FALSE
2. There are several people in the store.	TRUE	FALSE
3. The thief takes María's purse.	TRUE	FALSE
4. The thief wants Tony to give him food.	TRUE	FALSE
5. Tony calls the fire department.	TRUE	FALSE

Practice 2

Describe the pictures to a partner. What do you see? What are they wearing?

1.

2.

3.

 ## Listening

 Circle the appropriate response to the statement or question that you hear:

1. A. There is a fire.

   B. Someone had a heart attack.

   C. There is a car accident.

2. A. Call an ambulance.

   B. Call the police.

   C. Call the doctor.

3. A. Get a cup of coffee.

   B. Get the fire extinguisher.

   C. Get the wet floor sign.

4. A.

   B.

   C.

Writing

Describe the following people:

1. _____

   _____

2. _____

   _____

3. _____

   _____

 # Homework

Make sure that the smoke alarm in your house is working. Write the emergency and non-emergency numbers for the places listed below. Copy this chart and put it by your phone at home.

	EMERGENCY	NON-EMERGENCY
POLICE		
FIRE		
POISON CONTROL		
NEIGHBOR		

Pronunciation

 Homonyms are words in English that sound the same, but are spelled differently and have different meanings. Listen and repeat:

to, too, two	there, their, they're	our, hour	road, rode
hear, here	some, sum	clothes, close	ate, eight

With a partner, write sentences using each of the homonyms showing that you understand the difference in meanings. Share your sentences with the rest of the class.

Vocabulary

<u>Verbs</u>
to approach
to injure
to fall
to mop
to refuse
to run
to shop
to slip
to steal

<u>Nouns</u>
accident
ambulance

cafeteria
cashier
car accident
fight
fire extinguisher
heart attack
kitchen
mall
men's restroom
operator
robbery
security
purse
women's restroom

Fun Activity

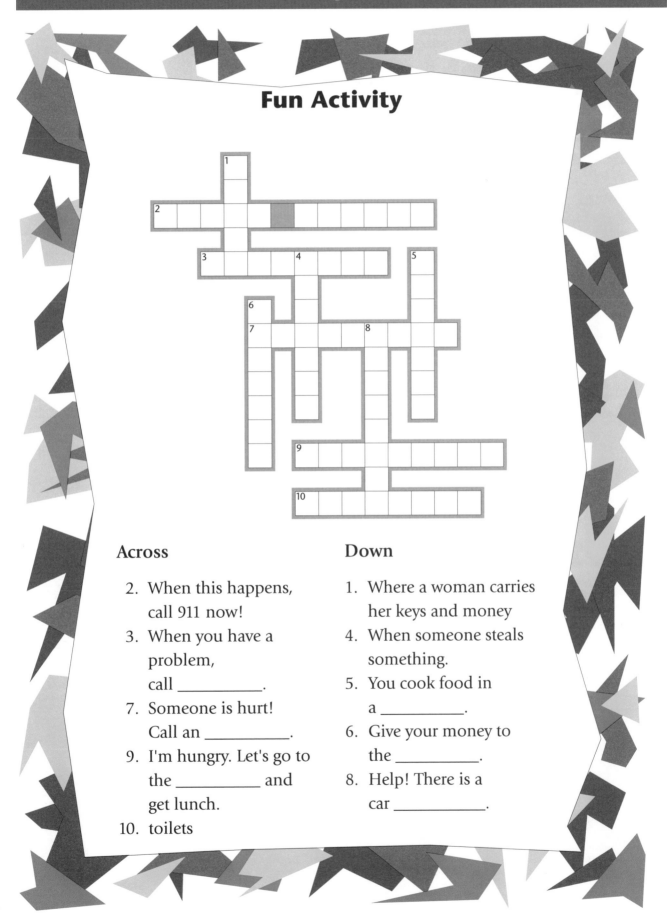

Across

2. When this happens, call 911 now!
3. When you have a problem, call _____.
7. Someone is hurt! Call an _____.
9. I'm hungry. Let's go to the _____ and get lunch.
10. toilets

Down

1. Where a woman carries her keys and money
4. When someone steals something.
5. You cook food in a _____.
6. Give your money to the _____.
8. Help! There is a car _____.

COMMUNICATION GOALS: Responding to safety warnings

Identifying safety items for protection

Are you OK?

Watch out!

Careful!

Look out!

 Talking

1. What do you see?
2. Where are they?
3. What are they saying?

Listening and Speaking

1. Listen
2. Listen and repeat
3. Practice with a partner

Nora and José are working in a factory. They work with chemicals and sometimes chemicals spill on the floor. They must wear protective boots.

José: I hate wearing these boots. They are ugly!

Nora: I know what you mean, but the rubber soles are necessary to keep us from slipping on a wet floor. My mother has to wear a hair net to work because she works in a restaurant as a cook. She doesn't like wearing it, but she has to follow the rules. The hair net keeps her hair from falling into the customer's food. If that happened, the customer would complain and she could lose her job!

José: WOW. I'm glad I don't have to wear a hair net. My son has to wear goggles to protect his eyes when he works. He works in manufacturing and must protect his eyes. Also, he has to wear earplugs because it gets loud in the manufacturing plant. So, I won't complain anymore about having to wear work shoes. They are keeping me safe!!

Nora: I agree.

Later in the day . . .

José: Nora, could you get me some tools?

Nora: Sure. What do you need?

José: I need a wrench, hammer and screwdriver. Also, don't forget a pair of protective gloves for my hands.

Nora: OK. I'll bring them after my break.

José: Thank you!

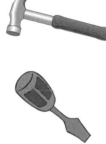

Matching

Draw a line from the word to the picture:

Hard hat

Hair net

Apron

Back brace

Gloves

Earplugs

Rubber boots

Safety goggles

Practice 1

Ask your partner these questions. If they wear something to protect themselves, ask for more details.

From what do you need protection:

From a spill?

From falling material?

From loud noises?

What do you use to protect your eyes?   From what?

What do you use to protect your head?   From what?

What do you use to protect your feet?   From what?

What do you use to protect your ears?   From what?

What do you use to protect your hands?   From what?

Reading

Read the following. Then answer the questions.

Mike is the safety officer for his factory. His job is to keep all the employees safe at the factory. He makes sure all the employees are wearing proper clothing and protection. He also makes sure everyone follows the safety rules. He writes reports everyday. This morning two people were smoking near the chemical storage room. He told them to stop. They could have caused a fire with toxic smoke.

Questions

1. Mike is the _____ for his factory.
   - A. supervisor
   - B. assembly line worker
   - C. safety officer
   - D. janitor

2. His job is to _____.
   - A. supervise the work on the factory floor.
   - B. get reports on problems.
   - C. assemble the product.
   - D. operate the machines.

3. What was the problem this morning?
   - A. Two people were smoking near the chemical storage room.
   - B. The machine broke.
   - C. The welding was not done correctly.
   - D. Mike could not find the screwdriver.

4. Why did Mike tell the people to stop smoking?
   - A. They were not allowed to smoke inside the factory.
   - B. The factory was closed.
   - C. Everyone left the factory.
   - D. They could have caused a fire with toxic smoke.

5. Why would everyone have to leave the building?
   - A. Toxic smoke makes people sick.
   - B. Cigarette smoking is not allowed in the factory.
   - C. The shift was finished.
   - D. The machine stopped working.

Listening

 Listen to the story. Then answer the questions.

1. Why was there an accident at work?

    A. The assembly line stopped.

    B. Someone unplugged the machine.

    C. John wasn't wearing his safety goggles.

2. Why did John go to the emergency medical office?

    A. They have coffee and donuts today.

    B. John hurt his eye.

    C. John hurt his leg.

3. What will the safety officer do after the machine is unplugged?

    A. Write a report.

    B. Go back to work.

    C. Go to lunch.

4. What will the safety officer do first?

    A. Help John to the emergency medical office.

    B. Write a report.

    C. Look at the machine to check that it is safe.

5. What will the safety officer do next?

    A. Help John to the emergency medical office.

    B. Write a report.

    C. Look at the machine to check that it is safe.

Writing

Look at the picture. Write three sentences about the safety clothing or safety protection she is wearing.

_____

_____

_____

 ## Homework

The command (imperative) form of the verb is always the infinitive minus the "to". For example:

to work = Work   to call = Call   to return = Return   to give = Give

Think about examples using these commands at home and at work. Be prepared to share some examples with the class.

attach	install	take off	stop	check	call
return	give	plug	unplug	assemble	operate
smoke	find	leave	finish	go	look
write	take	go back	get		

Vocabulary

Verbs

to allow
to assemble
to attach
to cause
to fly
to go back
to install
to leave
to operate
to plug
to receive
to take off
to unplug
to wear
to weld

Nouns

assembly line
automobile
chemicals
drill
engineering
factory
frame
hammer
janitor
pliers
procedure
safety goggles
safety officer
screwdriver
storage room

Fun Activity

Word Search

automobile drill factory hammer janitor
pliers apron gloves boots hairnet
procedure safety goggles screwdriver

```
h  a  m  m  e  r  i  y  o  c  p  b  q  z  j
u  h  a  i  r  n  e  t  s  m  l  o  a  g  h
w  k  f  j  g  b  d  f  o  o  i  o  p  y  d
v  f  a  c  t  o  r  y  x  n  e  t  r  s  s
s  o  l  y  d  x  f  e  s  k  r  s  o  d  j
i  m  v  e  l  r  h  c  x  d  s  x  n  r  r
p  r  o  c  e  d  u  r  e  z  q  v  c  i  w
t  o  i  d  r  l  b  e  u  l  k  s  x  l  t
p  s  l  g  t  g  v  f  n  w  d  r  d  l  c
t  e  d  e  s  c  r  e  w  d  r  i  v  e  r
m  d  a  u  t  o  m  o  b  i  l  e  b  p  g
g  w  s  l  f  q  l  t  j  a  n  i  t  o  r
s  a  f  e  t  y  g  o  g  g  l  e  s  w  r
v  v  j  c  s  s  g  l  o  v  e  s  h  x  i
s  q  f  v  l  n  h  r  b  m  m  e  r  b  f
```

Many verbs in English do not follow the regular pattern in the past tense. Practice using these verbs in a sentence. Use a dictionary if you need help.

Simple Form	Simple Past	Simple Form	Simple Past
begin	began	is	was
break	broke	know	knew
bring	brought	leave	left
buy	bought	lose	lost
come	came	make	made
cost	cost	meet	met
cut	cut	pay	paid
do	did	put	put
drink	drank	read	read
drive	drove	run	ran
eat	ate	say	said
fall	fell	see	saw
feel	felt	send	sent
find	found	shut	shut
forget	forgot	sit	sat
get	got	speak	spoke
give	gave	steal	stole
go	went	take	took
have	has	tell	told
hold	held	write	wrote
hurt	hurt		

Simple Present of the verb TO BE

I	am	an office worker.
you	are	a hospital worker.
he	is	a kitchen worker.
she	is	a construction worker.
it	is	a fast food worker.
we	are	tall, short, hungry, or tired.
they	are	from China.

Simple Past of the verb TO BE

I	was	
you	were	
he	was	tired yesterday
she	was	hungry an hour ago.
it	was	angry last week.
we	were	
they	were	

Simple Future

I		
you		
he		work tomorrow.
she	will	take a break now.
it		put on your goggles to protect your eyes.
we		
they		

Present Continuous

I	am	
you	are	
he	is	
she	is	working right now.
it	is	
we	are	
they	are	

Past Continuous

I	was	
you	were	
he	was	
she	was	working yesterday.
it	was	
we	were	
they	were	

Modals

I		
you		eat Pizza later.
he	will may can	study English tonight.
she	could might	go to Colombia next week.
it	must should	play soccer today.
we		
they		

Notes – Write new words

Notes – Write questions to ask your teacher or supervisor

_____

_____

_____

_____

_____

_____

_____

_____

_____

_____

_____

_____